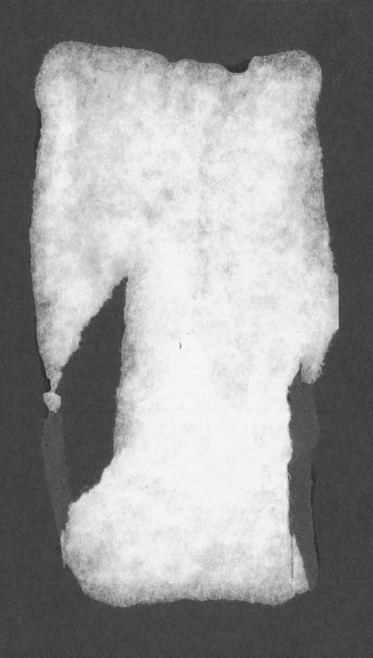

ASK ANY VEGETABLE

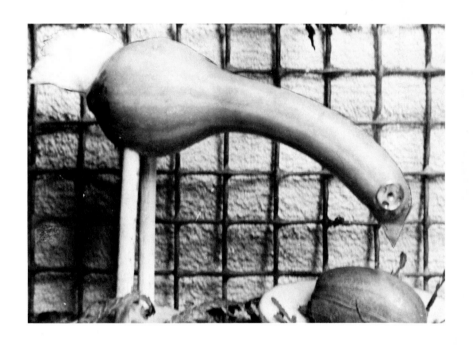

ASK ANY VEGETABLE

R. E. Eshmeyer

**Illustrated with Photographs
and Drawings by the Author**

Prentice-Hall, Inc. Englewood Cliffs, N.J.

Printed in the United States of America J

Prentice-Hall International, Inc., London
Prentice-Hall of Australia, Pty. Ltd., North Sydney
Prentice-Hall of Canada, Ltd., Toronto
Prentice-Hall of India Private Ltd., New Delhi
Prentice-Hall of Japan, Inc., Tokyo

Library of Congress Cataloging in Publication Data

Eshmeyer, Reinhart Ernest.
    Ask any vegetable.

    SUMMARY: Instructions for making various animals
and scenes using vegetables.
    1. Handicraft—Juvenile literature. 2. Vegetables
—Juvenile literature. [1. Handicraft.
2. Vegetables] I. Title.
TT160.E75   745.5   74–20969
ISBN 0–13–049759–2

The text for this book was set in 12 pt. Caledonia,
and the display type was set in Craw Modern
Bold, by the Spartan Typographers.

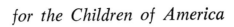

for the Children of America

FOREWORD

Some of nature's most pleasing and artistic shapes are to be found in our common vegetables. These forms, especially if we look for them, often remind us of animals. To look for such similarities is one of the best ways to develop the ability to observe— to see more in what we look at than a casual glance ever affords.

In using familiar vegetable and nuts in the making of animal forms we put our powers of imagination to practical use. The activities recommended here are stimulating and develop a desire for creativity. The practical working out of the details of the projects becomes far more entertaining than playing with any type of manufactured toy.

Children take naturally to what is suggested in this book. They feel a oneness with nature already, and once they get the general idea they achieve a new satisfaction in creating. Older people, too, have found enjoyment in doing these projects.

This book suggests using only vegetables of normal size and shape, not the freaks of nature. This is an important point. Look long at an ordinary gourd of any sort and it will suggest many things to you.

Gourds are hard vegetables and are not used for food. We now come to a group of what I call soft vegetables. These are used for food.

Once you get started seeing all sorts of forms in gourds you are going to wonder about yams, squashes, pickles, potatoes, carrots, and other vegetables. Because we need to conserve food we should take care not to damage any vegetables or let them rot in our arrangements.

This book is the result of many experiments, which do not require an outlay of much cash. The tools used here are found in almost any household: long-nose pliers, a small drill and bits, a hacksaw, and a pair of short-nose shears. We also use large pins or paper clips, and modeling clay.

We do suggest several activities in which soft vegetables are used: yams, a cucumber, a squash, and a potato. These can be used for an hour's sheer pleasure, and in such a way that they can still be used for food. When a person sees a different form of life in a yam, and can create that form with a few additions, this pleasure should be permitted, for the imagination is thus further developed.

Gourds, cornstalks, and maple seeds are materials frequently used, and some excellent permanent displays may be accomplished.

When a member of the family has completed an artistic arrangement, it can be used as a centerpiece at a meal or two so the creator of it receives the interest and encouragement of the family.

Special thanks to my photographic assistant, Mervin C. Dosh; to my wife, Elba, for her constant help; and to Clara Schroen, a fifth-grade teacher, for her invaluable suggestions.

R. E. Eshmeyer
East Lansing, Michigan

TABLE OF CONTENTS

Smaller Gourds

ASK
ANY
VEGETABLE

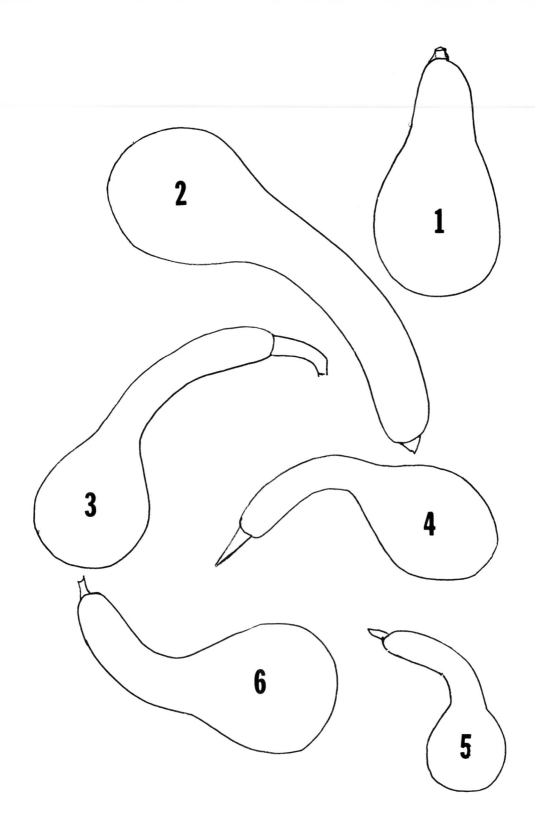

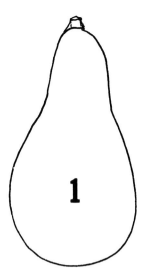

WHAT DO THE GOURDS
HAVE TO SAY?

Take a gourd in your hand and turn it every possible way you can think of to see if at any angle it reminds you of some other form in nature. Ask No. 1 what it would like to be. In the outline No. 1 reminds us of a rabbit that has its back turned toward us. All it needs is long ears.

Because gourds are some of nature's most beautiful forms many people like to have them in their homes, especially for decorations around Thanksgiving time. Because of their popularity they are sold both in farmers' and city markets.

Gourds have many more shapes and sizes than the outlines show, and there is no end to what you can make with them. Study the shapes. The colors remain for a long time, but they will eventually fade. A faded gourd can be painted in gaudy colors.

In the early days of our country gourds were used for dippers and other containers because they are strong and last for a long, long time. Even today an elderly woman may keep a gourd in her sewing basket to stretch over it a sock that needs darning.

We will use all six of the forms shown as we go along, but right now let's see what we can do with No. 1.

LAMP

In this simple project you can catch the excitement of working with gourds.

Place a wad of modeling clay on a piece of waxed paper. The clay should be well worked so that it is pliable.

Push the No. 1 gourd "bottom" into the clay. Press the clay against the gourd to make it sit more solidly.

Leaving just the part of the paper that touches the clay, cut away the rest of the paper. The gourd should now stand straight up. The paper bottom will protect anything you may want to set it on.

If you have a tulip or tuliplike flower, use it for a lampshade, as I did here. If no flowers are available for this purpose, use a pointed paper cup (or make one). When you have decided how far you want the paper cup to hang over, mark the place with a pencil. Remove the cup and flatten it. Draw scallops on the edge and cut off what you don't want.

You may want to paint the shade. Perhaps the gourd, too.

Use your own ideas to improve on this lamp. Use your imagination. Have fun.

6

RABBIT

Gourd No. 1 can also be used to create a rabbit. Three things are necessary: (1) we must tilt the rabbit so that it will sit up; (2) we must give it some long ears; (3) we must give it a tail.

Look at the sketch of the maple seeds (Fig. 1). These are from a Norway maple, and seem to be the largest, but all maple seeds make good ears. Maple seeds of various kinds drop all summer long, and you can even find them in winter and spring under dead leaves.

Maple seeds grow in pairs (Fig. 1). They have a hard knob that houses the seed; a wing, which helps the wind to carry it to a new place where it can become a tree. Notice that along one side of each wing there is a heavy rib, which holds the flimsy part of the wing together. The dotted lines (Fig. 2) show where the seeds are to be cut off.

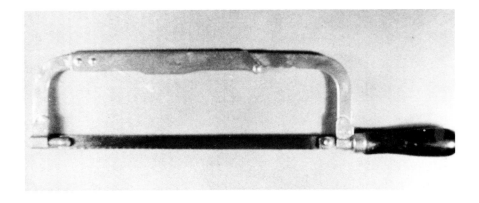

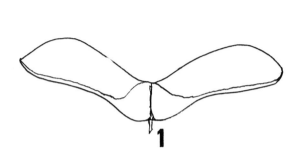
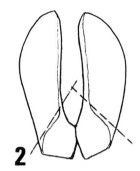

Cut on dotted line

To make the rabbit lean forward the easiest way is to hold a gourd firmly in a wad of clay and saw off a piece of the bottom at an angle, shown in Figs. 3 and 4. Use a hacksaw. Nearly every household has one of these useful tools.

The easiest way to affix the ears is to make a saw cut through the top (Fig. 5). See how the dotted line here comes from the tail to between the ears. Now you can tell where the saw cut for the ears must go. Set the ears in place with clay.

Put the tail on last. Paint the spot with glue and hold a wad of cotton on it for a minute or so.

You'll need a platform or stage. See a simple one in Fig. 5. But look ahead, just in case you want to make a better one, to page **31**. This one gives you room enough to set grass and weeds around the rabbit.

Paint the rabbit if you wish.

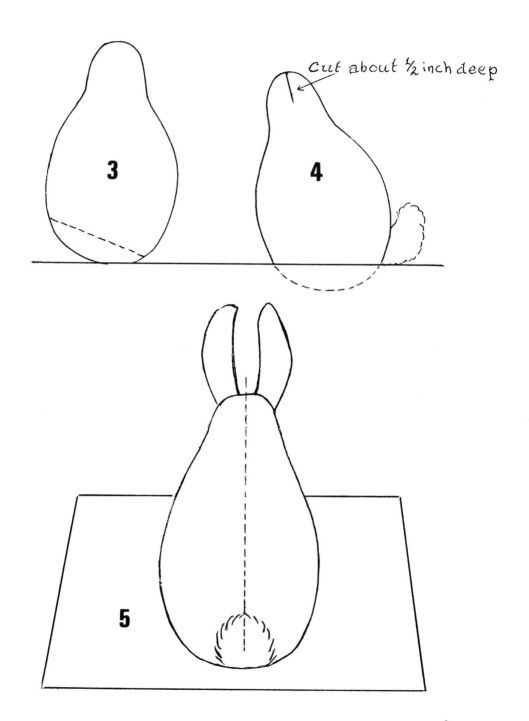

Cut about ½ inch deep

3

4

5

9

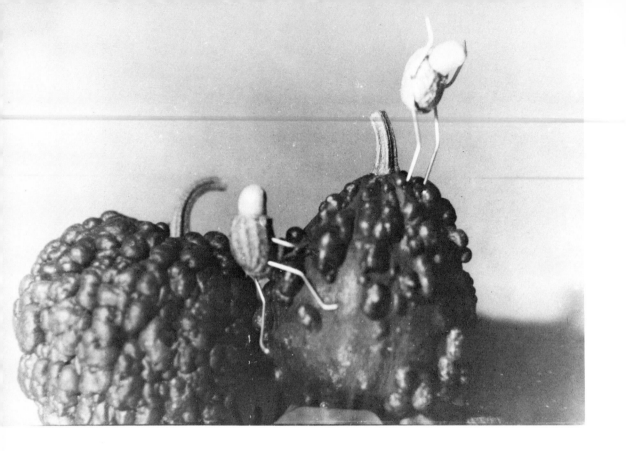

FLOWERPOT

Another project you can do with gourd No. 1 is to make a flowerpot. Study the sketch.

If the gourd is dry the flowerpot can be used. Just fill it with good soil and plant a flower. Even if the gourd is still green it ought to work. Then, when it gets dry, you can paint it the color you want.

If you can handle the hacksaw by now and have but one gourd to work on, cut a ring out of the top of the gourd. See sketch. Make the top cut first, marked Cut 1. Now make Cut 2 about a quarter inch down. You now have a ring and a pot. Set the pot on the ring and pack the underside with clay.

10

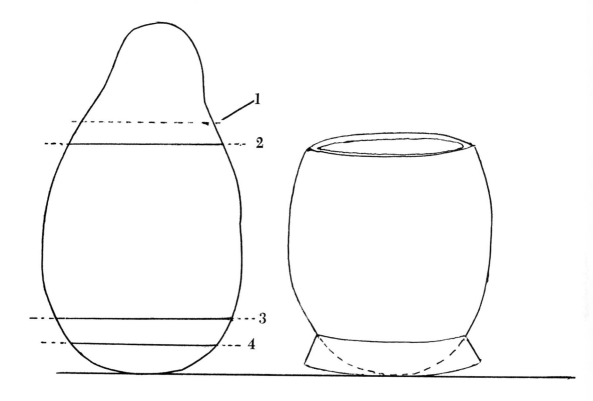

If you have two gourds of the same size you may decide to make a larger ring from the bottom of one of the gourds. See Cuts 3 and 4 in sketch.

When the pot is ready it can be painted with almost any kind of paint you have on hand—if the gourd is dry.

If you don't succeed with the ring idea you can set up the pot in the same way the lamp was made to stand. You can change to a ring later if you wish to make more pots and have had more practice with the hacksaw.

There are gourds, and very pretty ones, that naturally stand upright. See the photograph. (Ignore the "peanut people" here, for we will meet them later.) If you are lucky enough to find such gourds, all you need do to make a flowerpot is to cut off the tops.

12

PENGUINS

No. 1 gourd is such an interesting shape that we just can't leave it yet. There are gourds of this general form which are skinnier through their bodies than some we have been working with. The skinny ones make good penguins.

Select two gourds. Saw off enough of the bottom to make them stand.

Paint their backs black and their front parts white. Look at a picture of a penguin in a book if you need a reminder of just how a penguin looks.

When the paint is dry drill a small hole where the beak is to be.

For the beak use part of the bottom end of a feather shaft.

Add the eyes (see page 14). Use glue to stick them on.

Surround the penguins with broken pieces of styrofoam, which looks like ice.

Inexpensive eyes with moving black pupils, in large and small sizes, are available in nearly all arts and crafts departments of large stores as well as in stores specializing in crafts.

On page 7 you will see a sketch of a rabbit sitting on a platform made of just a piece of cardboard. You might want to make a simple stage like this for your penguins, but look ahead to page 31. You might want to make a real stage like the one pictured there.

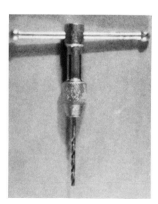

A brace and bits for drilling holes.

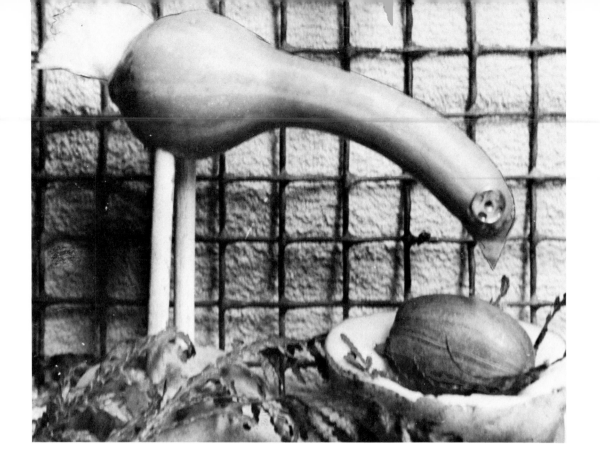

BIRD

This bird is a No. 2 gourd. The long, heavy neck and small body make us wonder what kind of bird it is. I have never seen one like it. It is an imaginary bird.

By the expression on its face one would suppose that the bird just can't understand how it could possibly lay such a big egg.

The bird's legs are sucker sticks. Thin wooden rods called dowels can be bought at a hardware store in about three-foot lengths. One of these dowels one-quarter-inch thick would provide many legs for you.

The holes you drill in the gourd must also be a quarter inch in diameter. Cut the legs long enough so they reach to the inside top of the bird.

The tail is made of cotton; the eye here is part of a clasp (a glass eye, such as you can buy in packets, might be better); the nest is a hollowed-out potato (this would wilt before long, so it would be better to use the bottom of a large gourd); the egg is a pecan.

The bird stands in a lump of clay on which bits of foliage have been laid.

The stage has a back to it. Cloth was stretched over the back, and a piece of poultry wire was placed in front of it to make it seem as though the bird is in a zoo. (See page 31 for more on stage).

15

18

FRIGHTENED GOOSE

This is a No. 4 gourd. The little stage has a cloth backdrop. There is a strip of clay along the back used to hold weed stems. Behind the goose is a flimsy bush made of steel wool. On the stage floor is a piece of old carpet strewn with bits of weeds. Among the litter is a shiny object that frightened the goose.

The bill of the goose is the gourd's natural stem. The wings are wooden. If you find it hard to get wooden spoons, you can make the wings out of cardboard. The eye was put on last.

Mark two places on the back of the goose where you want the wings to go. Drill small holes at each end of the marks, and a few between, then break out what is left between. Fit the wings, then lay them aside.

The big job is to balance the goose on its legs. The leg to the back is a long nail. Put a mark on the goose where the leg is to go, then drill a hole a little smaller than the nail leg. Stick the nail through the floor of the stage.

Before you push the goose on the nail make another hole in the goose for the other leg. Use a feather shaft, leaving enough plume at the bottom to resemble a webbed foot. Now put it all together. Paste on the eye. Put a shiny piece of metal in front of the goose, but not too close to it.

This makes a very interesting and pretty piece of gourd art, and you can accomplish it if you stick with it. It would be best to place it on a larger stage such as the one suggested on page 31.

20

SWAN

This is a No. 5 gourd.

When spring came the keeper of the park built a floating nest for the swans who lived in the pond.

To make the little hut for the nest it is best to start with a cardboard box about ½ x 4 x 4 inches. Use only the lid. The ½ inch suggested could be larger or smaller. The idea is that it will appear to keep the brooder hut off the water. If your box is too long cut part of the middle off and push the two end pieces together. The unevenness where the two parts are joined will not matter.

Now attach a piece of cardboard on sides and back. This piece should be scored at two places and each section should be 4 x 4 inches. So, you will cut the cardboard 4 x 12 inches and mark off 4 inches from each end. Bend at the scoring marks and drape the piece around or inside the box lid you have ready for it.

Now measure for the kind of roof you want, score the center, and put the roof in place. If you want to close in the opening at the back of the hut it will be fine, but not really necessary.

Fill the nest part with steel wool or corn silk, place the swan into it, and set the whole thing on a mirror, or a sheet of shiny metal.

The bill is the natural stem of the gourd. The eye you already know about. Use a clay bank and stick a few plants into it.

LITTLE INDIANS

Make a cornstalk or other type of log for the boys to sit on. They are in the woods warming up while their fathers are fishing. Arrange cornstalks to represent trees. Build a fire with thin cornstalk and keep a place behind the fire where you can turn on a small flashlight when you want to show the scene to friends.

To make the boys' heads look round use clay. Also, add clay to round out their shoulders. If you want to show the arms as in the picture do it with clay.

Stick a few feathers behind a headband.

Since the fire would put the boys in shadow, you might paint them black. When the paint dries you can add a few decorative strokes across the shoulders with light paint.

How can you make the boys sit up? Drive three nails into them (as in a three-legged stool) and cover what shows with a bit of cornhusk.

This activity may make you think of a lot more things you can do with No. 1 gourds.

FOX AND CRANE

This makes an interesting conversation piece at the lunch table. Here the fox is invited to have lunch with the crane, but he can't get at the food because it is served in a tall vaselike dish. The fox is very hungry and very disappointed, as you can see.

But, if you remember the fable, it served him right, because he had first invited the crane to lunch and had served everything on flat plates, and the poor bird couldn't get at the food.

The gourd used for the crane is a No. 3 form. The bill is a piece of feather shaft. The tall vase is a No. 1 gourd with the top cut off.

The fox was made of a small immature No. 1 gourd, with clay on the thin end into which ears and eyes were stuck. A bit of cotton was pasted over the body to resemble fur, and the bushy tail was built up of strands of corn silk. The fox's ears are feather-shaft ends.

Flowers and weed stems help to set off this outdoor lunch.

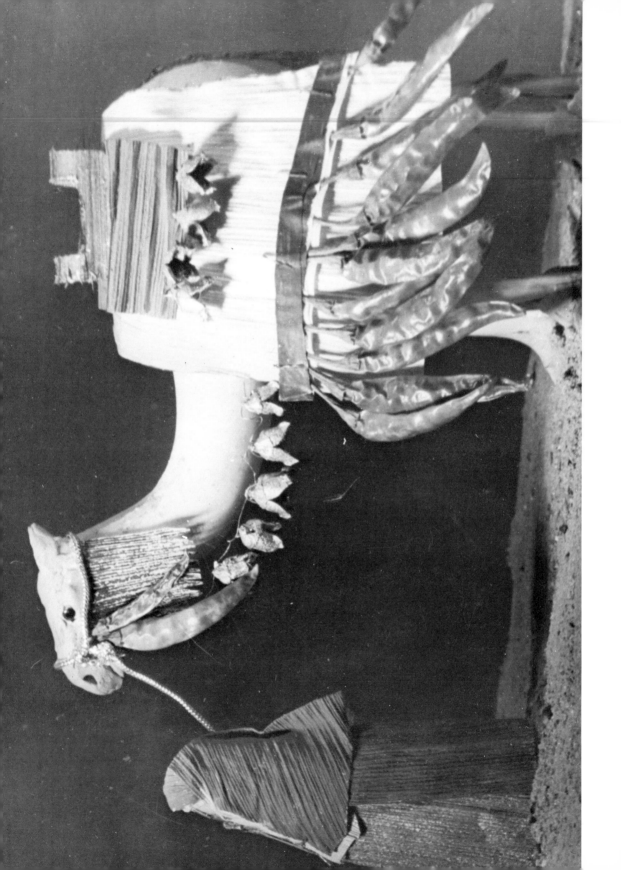

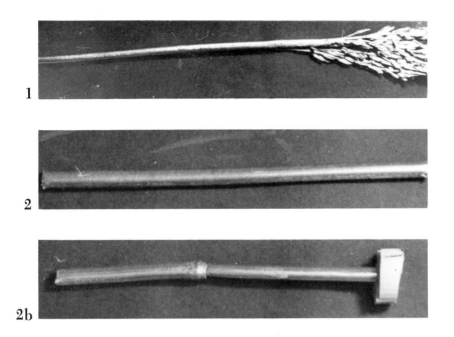

1

2

2b

CAMEL

The camel is a No. 6 gourd. Use clay in making the head. If
you look closely you will see a bump on the forehead. This bump
is actually the end of the gourd. So all you really need to do is
put on the nose part and the ears. Note the slant of the nose and
see the nostril. Use a glass eye.

For a blanket use cornhusk such as you see around the ear in
Fig. 4. The saddle was cut out of a larger piece of cornstalk than
you see in Fig. 3. Under the saddle is more cornhusk with stripes

27

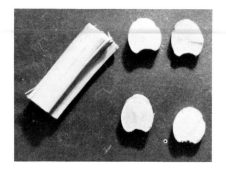

3   4

painted on it. The special decorations dangling from the blanket are little red peppers, and the gilded bells are the cones of the witchhazel shrub. The man is a small gourd sawed off at the bottom to make him stand. His dress is cornhusk and was painted.

The legs are cornstalk. Fig. 1 shows part of the top section of a cornstalk, which sprouts the tassel. Fig. 2 was cut off of it. Fig. 2 has a little of the top section plus a joint and part of the second section of the stalk. To this is attached a foot.

Fig. 3 shows four feet. They are headed up. The heavy chunk near them shows that the larger sections of cornstalk have a groove. This groove can make a camel's foot look like it has two toes (a cloven hoof) like a cow. Pack a little clay around the top of the foot to connect it to the stalk leg.

It would be good to show a knee, as in Fig. 2b, but if your blanket fringe comes below the knee a straight leg (dowel or cornstalk) is all right.

Mark four spots on the camel body where the legs are to go. Press an ice pick or large nail into the spot to make a dent. This will make it easier to get the drilling bit started. Drill as large a hole as you need for the legs and let them come into the inside top of the gourd.

Put sand on the stage (see page 31) floor to represent the desert.

28

1

NUT-CUP PLACE-CARD HOLDER

If you are planning a party and would like to make some special nut-cup place-card holders, here is an idea.

Select the number of gourds you will need. Cut off the bottoms, for these nut cups must stand straight up; don't cut them off at an angle. Now make a saw cut at the top, as you did for the rabbit. This will hold the name card. If you do not want the ears of this rabbit to come against the card make another saw cut as marked on Fig. 1.

Now scrape out the insides of the gourds and discard along with the bottoms you sawed off. Clean up your work space before going ahead.

Shove a pointed paper clip into each gourd and trim off the extra paper that sticks out at the bottom.

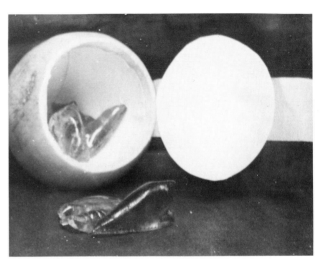

2

Set each gourd separately on a piece of clean, thin cardboard and draw a line around it. This becomes the cover (see Fig. 3). Do not mix up these covers for the gourds won't be shaped exactly alike and the covers won't fit.

With a strip of tape get each cover in its own place, but do not fasten both ends until you have filled the cups with nuts and candy. See Fig. 3 to decide where the tape is to go, so that the one end that shows will be covered with the tail.

Close the cover. Insert the maple-seed ears. Be sure the name is on each card before you insert it in the slot. Paint the spot with glue where the tail is to go, and hold a wad of cotton on the glued area for a minute or so to make sure it is firmly attached.

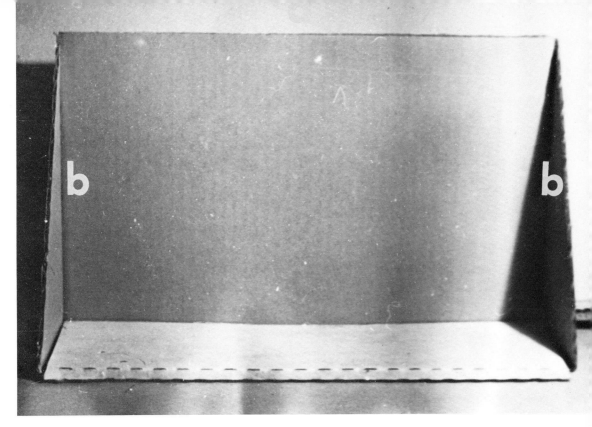

1

THE STAGE

A stage provides a setting for your craft projects and helps you plan your arrangements. Making a different background for each animal you create is another project in itself and calls on your imagination, too.

A real stage is more satisfactory than the flat cardboard platforms we've been talking about. It is easy to make.

Fig. 1 shows part of a well-made cardboard box. I used only the lid. The lid measured 3 x 12 x 14 inches. I measured off on the inside of one end of the lid just 7 inches. The other side the same. Then I drew a line from one mark to the other and cut the box in two on that line.

2   3

Then I drew a line from the ends of the cut I had just made down to the bottom outside corners (see **b**). I cut the outside pieces off. They are already off in the photograph.

Next I cut a piece of cardboard 7 inches wide and 11 inches long to fit into the stage to extend the stage floor. A carpet can be placed over this floor.

The carpet was intended for the outdoor setting for the goose that is seen on page 19. You will want to change the floor of the stage many times, but the stage itself will last and last.

You can make a stage out of any box. Fig. 2 shows the end of a shoe box.

If you have no box but have a piece of cardboard, you can make a stage from scratch. See Fig. 3. Where the cardboard is to be bent it must be scored to make it bend at the line you make. Place a ruler on the lines and run a blunt instrument along the ruler to dent the cardboard. But do not cut into it.

Part II Larger Gourds

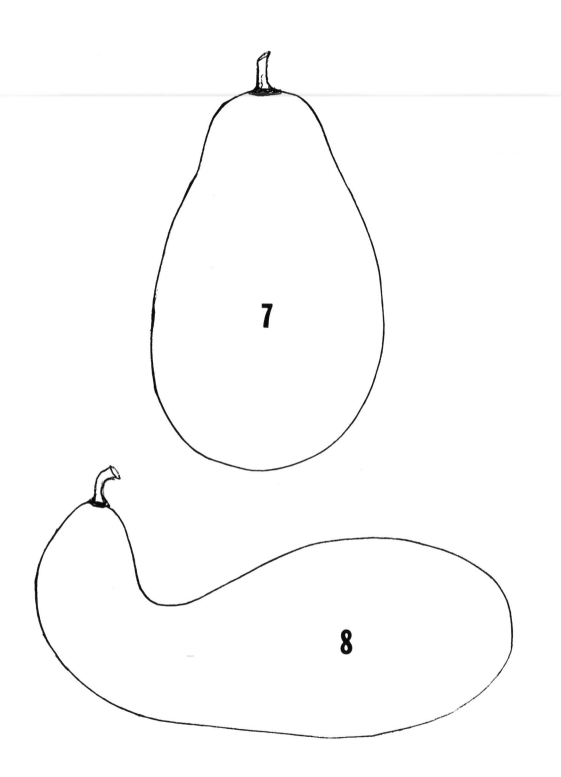

Among the larger gourds we find forms similar to some of the six smaller ones we've been working with. But something has been added besides size, and that is the fascinating "bumps" all over them. Usually these gourds are in solid colors, from bright yellow to red orange. They are some of nature's most attractive creations.

No. 7 is a very pretty yellow gourd. It would make an excellent flowerpot. Or, if only a little of the top were sawed off it would make an exciting vase for blue flowers.

The owl (page 41) is one of the most attractive displays of all. It too is a No. 7 gourd.

No. 8 is a larger gourd than No. 7 and is also covered with smooth bumps, which makes it very attractive. Its shape lends itself to many kinds of arrangements. We will do four.

If you can find only one No. 8 gourd you will have to choose what you wish to make with it. If you do a good job you will enjoy the results very much. Your artistic creation will last a long time. When the colors fade you can paint it again.

OWL

When we first saw No. 7 at the market I immediately thought of an owl. It just had to be an owl!

A barn owl often spends its daytime sleeping hours in a barn. So, I nailed a few boards together and made a place for the owl to sleep.

Its horns are fashioned out of modeling clay. It has large, scary eyes. (For eyes see page 14.)

The beak is the bottom end of a large feather shaft.

The talons are bent pins covered with clay.

Feathers and bits of bone suggest that the owl has been feeding, although in the case of small rodents and birds the owl swallows everything.

I didn't need to fasten this owl down in any way, for it stood straight up in the corner I'd made for it.

GRASSHOPPER

I "saw" the grasshopper in the big, bright yellow No. 8 gourd, but I didn't know how to begin. The reason for this was that I really didn't know what a grasshopper looks like.

Our big dictionary has many illustrations. I looked up the word "grasshopper," and I found a drawing of one. You can find many illustrations in any dictionary.

For the big jumping legs I used cornstalk, and for the front legs I used horsetail weed, although thick cornstalk would have done just as well. I fastened the legs on with small nails. The wing is a piece of cornhusk.

The antennae are small seed pods for which I haven't found a name. There are many useful weed heads and pods which one may use, and it isn't too important to know the names of them.

The eye is the usual glass eye, the larger size.

The greenery in the back came from a flowerpot. Dried grass and weed stems, as well as small leaves, can be painted green, and they will last a very long time.

Like Dinny (page 48), the big grasshopper is a dandy. It takes time and patience to do one, but stay with it and you'll succeed, because it's really a lot of fun.

44

PROUD SWAN

This No. 8 gourd is easily turned into a swan if you work carefully.

Make up an attractive stage on a mirror or shiny metal. Use clay in the background so you can anchor some dense grass. Corn silk dries and can be used for grass.

Saw the bottom off the gourd, as shown. This will make it stand up without a prop.

Leave the natural stem but carve it to a point. If you happen to knock it off, finish the carving and then paste it on again.

Paint the whole body white. When the paint is thoroughly dry add the wing. Use your own judgment about the kind of leaf you want to use. You might prefer a thin cardboard cut to a point, and, of course, painted white.

Since you can now get into the inside of the gourd you can use a needle and fasten the wing on with thread. Drill tiny holes and sew the wing on like a button. Farther up from the "stem" you can use glue to help hold the wing in place.

GOLDEN PHEASANT

This No. 8 gourd was again a bright yellow. I saw in it the making of a pheasant. All it needed was a bit of clay for the comb and wattle, which would be painted red.

When you do something on your own you may come to puzzling problems as I did in this case. I took the problems one at a time. The biggest one was making the bird stand up. It was a rather heavy gourd and always wanted to fall down.

The way to make it stand up is to use a dowel or other strong stick about 8 inches long. This stick should be wood so you can cut off what may not be needed. Place a board under the stage floor and drill a quarter-inch hole almost all the way through. Fit the dowel into it. Hold the gourd against the upright dowel and judge what length the dowel should be if you pushed it through a hole in the gourd and all the way into the back. Now drill a hole in the gourd and push the gourd over the dowel. It would help if you sharpened the dowel at the top in a pencil sharpener. Get this one leg solid and you can make another leg to match, which will not need to go into the wood floor.

The tail was the next problem. I finally decided on some ornamental grass which I bought at a farmers' market.

The pheasant is looking at its feed, which is real corn. The floor of its cage is strewn with ordinary dirt.

If you set up some cornstalk trees in the back you may not need a fence at all. Always use your own ideas.

48

DINNY

This is another No. 8 gourd. Here the stage was set with trees. The idea was to brace Dinny against one to make him stand up. He is a bright orange dinosaur.

Cornstalks and sunflower stalks were used for trees, and some potted plants were used to add green.

Cornstalks were used for the large hind legs. They were attached to the body with nails, and some corn-leaf parts were used to cover the nailheads.

The front legs, which could easily have been made of cornstalk, were made of horsetail weed which I'd picked up on a trip. (I always look for new things to use, and suggest that you do the same.)

The front legs were also fastened to a tree. It is tricky to make Dinny stand up like that, but patience will succeed.

The natural stem of the gourd was carved to a point. The eye was glass but this was before I learned about the new moving eyes I've been telling you about.

The rest of the arrangement is easy except for the plates of armor along Dinny's back. These are the three-cornered (triangular) bits of metal called glaziers' points. They are used to fasten down window glass before putty is applied. I set these into Dinny's back at an angle, using pliers and carefully pushing with all my strength. It would be better to first carve in a groove with a sharp tool of some sort, being careful not to get hurt.

It's a great satisfaction to see the finished scene, but it takes patience to produce it however simple it may look.

50

INSIDE A GOURD

Make a house, garage, or shed out of a gourd. The house you see in the picture is a smooth, almost white gourd about 4½ inches long. (We will call this a No. 9 gourd, and we will use one more like it.)

The opening in this house or shed is about 2¼ inches square. There is a hole in the back through which I sent the light from a flashlight. A higher window in the back might have been better.

For the front opening cut out a 2-inch square of paper. Lay this on the gourd and draw a line around it. Now saw along each of the four sides of the square with a hacksaw. Hold the gourd down on a lump of clay, and cut the lines as far as you dare without running over the corners.

Now take the blade out of the saw and wrap rag around it up to 1 inch from one end. Use this 1 inch of blade to finish the cuts at the corners. This means you must shove the blade into the gourd and cut straight up and down. If you run over the line it will show, and you won't be able to do much about it.

You may decide against a hole in the lower part of the back but may want a window higher up. Use your own ideas.

Gourds have been used as wren houses and as bird feeders. In olden times they were used for dippers. But right now we are interested in exploring the gourd interiors for our artistic purpose. If you can't find a suitable gourd for an interior, perhaps you can find a small pumpkin, but this won't keep very long.

51

YAM ROOSTER

The yam rooster strikes me as a beautiful thing, and it's easy enough to do.

Clay was used to build out the head and to make a place for the clothespin beak. (You can't use a whole clothespin, but only the ends.)

Mold a thin layer of clay for the comb and wattle. Paint them red. Set the eye.

The hard part was to find a suitable tail. What do you think the tail was made of? After many tries it was found that the brown skins of a large onion did very well.

If you can't find chicken wire for the fence, do without it. Even sticks across the front of the stage will keep that rooster in.

There are weed bits on the floor. The "bread" is bits of styrofoam.

Once you've shown your family or friends your creation of a yam rooster, better take it down, clean the yam, and return it to the refrigerator.

NESTING HEN

Our first study in this section is a large squash. It is called a Hubbard squash. I carved its stem into a beak, added a clay comb and wattle, and, presto, all that was left to do was place an eye and a nest for this hen to sit in. My family seemed to like it very much but I did not keep it very long as a hen on a nest because we had bought the squash to eat.

My work on the hen did not hurt the squash at all, and we all had fun before we ate it.

For the hen, paint the bill yellow, and the clay comb and wattle red.

HATCHING CHICK

The egg here was a large smooth almost white gourd like the one used on page 50.

Zigzag a line around the middle of the gourd. Cut as far down as you dare on each part of the line. Now wrap the saw blade with rag, all but about an inch and finish the job. Clean out the two parts of the gourd.

The chick is a No. 6 gourd. Clay was used to build out the face. It is clay that holds the pieces of clothespin that make the bill.

Before bill and eyes are added paint the whole chick with a thinned glue and roll it in cotton. When dry, smooth out the cotton, stick in the bill and eyes, and set the chick in the eggshell as shown.

In the picture, shredded green tissue paper was used to suggest a nest.

Use your own ideas. This project gives you good results for not too much or too difficult work.

Part III Soft Vegetables

HARE AND TORTOISE

This scene pictures the start of the famous race between the hare and the tortoise, or the rabbit and the turtle.

The arrangement, as the ones before this, is put together with easy-to-get vegetables. The trees are carrots. The big rock is a potato. The "sticks" are very thin spaghetti. It is a woods scene with the ground covered with dead leaves.

The peanut rabbit has a few props under it to make it stand up. Bits of toothpick would be fine for this. The rabbit's ears are ash-tree seeds, but maple seeds would do just as well.

The tortoise may be very easy to get, or very hard, depending on whether or not you have a horse chestnut or buckeye tree growing near you. The tortoise is a horse chestnut. These drop from the tree in the fall. They are a beautiful brown and are very shiny. Growing two or three in a pod, they usually have one flat side such as the one I used here. I did nothing to this horse chestnut except place it in the scene beside the rabbit.

Once you see what needs to be done there is no need of spoiling the carrots or the potato. These should be used for food. You can make trees out of cornstalk and use a real rock in place of the potato.

If you do use carrots and a potato put them in last. Show the display to your family or friends and then remove the edibles.

INQUISITIVE CUCUMBER

You'd hardly buy this poorly formed cucumber at the market, but if you have your own garden you might find one.

The stage floor here is a piece of bright metal, but a mirror could be used. (Polished metal makes no double image as a mirror will.) On the back of the stage I placed an odd piece of driftwood I happened to have. You can think up a suitable background. Use some clay into which to stick weed stems and perhaps a little steel wool here and there.

The bird is wondering about the acorn cap in front of it. It is standing on a soft clay island at the edge of the pool. Its legs are made of the kind of wire florists use, but dowel sticks would do as well. If you prefer thin legs perhaps you can find some wire.

The bird wears a kind of crown on its head—part of the old stem of the cucumber.

The eye is one of the kind bought at craft stores. It is possible, of course, to use a small button, especially a white one.

You could add a tail if you think it would improve the funny bird, but this one had part of the old cucumber blossom left on it right where the tail should be, and I thought this was enough.

RESTING SEA LIONS

These sea lions basking in the sun seem to be very contented. They are lying on a cake of styrofoam "ice."

All you need add to them are flippers and eyes. In the picture the flippers are wooden spoons. If you find these hard to get you can use plastic ones. Cut off most of the handles and push them into the yams.

The chunks of ice seem to tell us that there's a hole in the ice nearby through which the sea lions probably came.

Yams are excellent food. No matter how much your creation of the sea lion arrangement may be admired, it is important to save the yams for cooking.

64

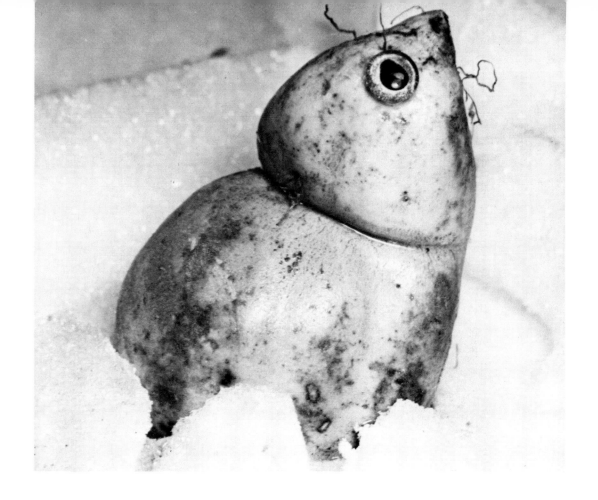

BABY SEAL

The little seal seems to be saying, "Good morning, world," as though it was its first look.

The "beard" is the yam's own natural roots, and was not even trimmed. In fact, nothing was changed on the yam at all except to give the seal an eye.

The ice is styrofoam.

This is one of the most interesting yams I have seen, and now that you have studied a few arrangements, it will make you look wonderingly when you see a bin of them.

Once you have made the baby seal, show it off to the family, then return the yam to the refrigerator. It will taste good later on.

PICKLE WORM

The pickle in the picture was about 4 inches long. Eyes and antennae were added. The antennae are pins.

Cornstalk trees are in the background. Grape leaves cover the foreground.

It's very simple to do, but it's quite a scary worm, don't you agree?

FOX AND CROW

This scene is based on the fable of the sly fox who couldn't reach the juicy grapes he longed for. He saw that the crow could get at them easily and was enjoying a feast. So the fox got the brilliant idea of telling the crow that she had a beautiful voice and that he would like to hear her sing. If the crow opened her mouth to sing she would drop the bunch of grapes she was feeding on.

The fox is a No. 1 gourd with the bottom sawed off, as you did with the rabbit, to make it sit up. The ears are small maple seeds. The bushy tail was fashioned from steel wool. The stage floor is covered with chips of bark and dry leaves.

The trees are the only edible vegetables used here. They are carrots. The grapevine wound around one of them is heavy twine.

It is worthwhile doing this pleasant scene even if you display it only once. But, if you want to keep it set up, you can use cornstalk in place of the carrots.

The grapes showing at the top could be anything you can find that resembles grapes enough to convey the message.

Part IV
Peanuts and Other Nuts

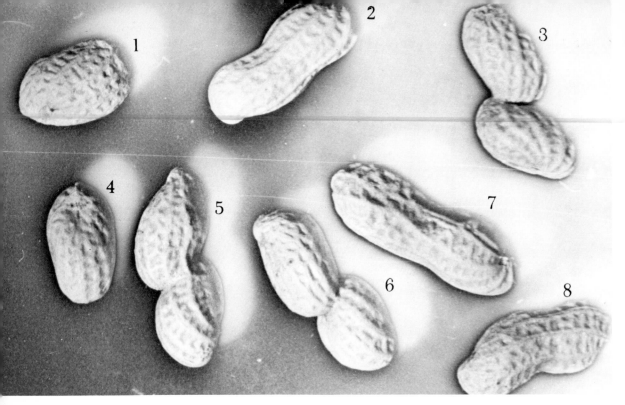

ABOUT PEANUTS

Study the pictures of the eight peanuts. It is very important that we select the proper shape for the particular purpose we have in mind.

Nos. 1 and 4 are single-kernel peanuts. You will soon come upon arrangements in which the single-kernel peanut is used, and you will see that a double-kernel nut could not be used as well in these cases. (See pages 75 and 111)

Nos. 2 and 7 have special uses, too, and we use them later in five arrangements.

Nos. 3, 5, 6, and 8 are best for peanut "people." No. 3 was used for the peanut-man sketch on page 72.

The pins are shown only to remind you of the importance of pins in this art. These are not actual size even for regular pins,

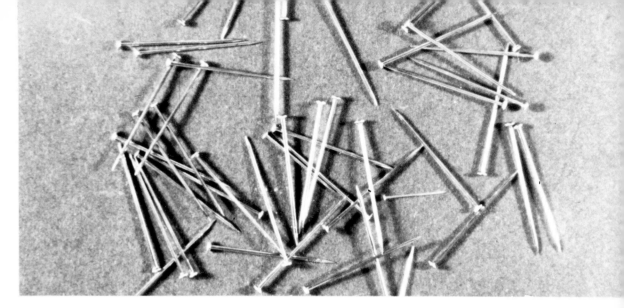

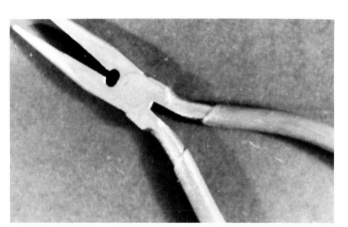

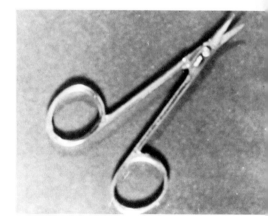

but they are sturdier than ordinary pins. If you can get them, use pins about 1¼ inches long.

The tiny shears are used to cut the peanut shell. Do not try to use a razor blade or a knife; they are dangerous and will not work anyhow. Just stick a hole into the peanut, with the shears, below the line on which you want to cut, rather than piercing the peanut wall right on the line. You will soon learn why when you make a wrong start. Go slow and easy and you will do a good job.

The pliers are the long-nose type. You will be needing these to bend pins or paper clips.

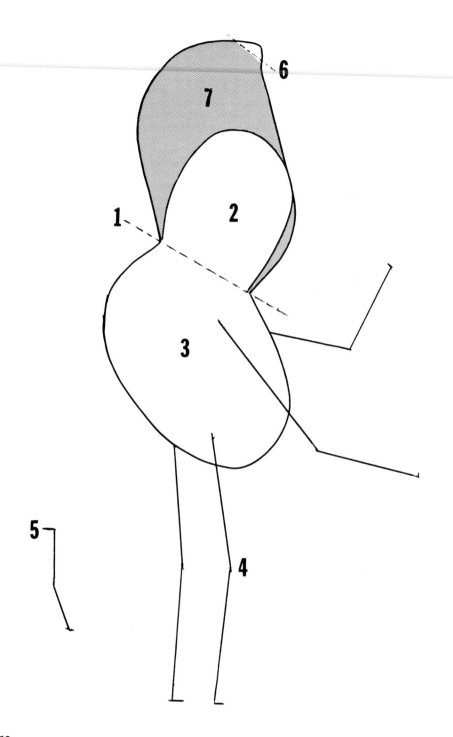

72

PEANUT MAN

Cut the peanut in two at the dotted line (see 1). Use short-bladed shears. Instead of starting the cut right on the line begin above it so you don't mar the edge of the body part.

The kernel head of the peanut man is shown in 2. If the kernel in the top was not harmed when you made the cut, you may find that it fits into the body part to make the head. If this does not work find a new head in another peanut. You may need to work away some of the kernel that remains in the body part. Should you work away too much, use clay to make the head fit.

The man's body is shown in 3. Arms and legs are stuck into it.

The arms and legs are very slightly bent to show where the elbows and knees are as well as to show the direction in which the man is headed (see 4). Hands and feet can be made by bending just the end of the clip a tiny bit. If pins are being used the heads will become hands and feet.

To bend a large pin or paper clip use a long-nose pliers. If you use a large pin it will be easier to push the point through the shell. Make the point about a quarter-inch long (see 5). Be sure to bend the pin or clip at a square angle, as in 5.

If you want to use a hat for your man cut the tip (6) off the peanut and glue it to a rounded piece of wrapping paper.

When you have removed the part for the hat you will have no further use for the rest of part 7.

Raw (unroasted) peanuts have white kernels. Also, if you use raw peanuts you will not be tempted to eat them.

Note that in the sketch we used peanut No. 3.

RACER

The horse has a one-kernel peanut body.

The cart is also a one-kernel peanut body.

The horse's mane is part of a feather. So is the tail.

The head of the horse—you'd never guess—is a grapefruit seed. It is joined to the body with a piece of heavy feather shaft.

The legs are pins. They are bent in such a way as to indicate speed. Nothing else in the picture gives you the impression of speed.

The shaves, which are strapped to the body with a narrow piece of cellophane tape (blackened), are a wire bent to a U shape. A twist at the bottom of the U makes it easy to attach them through a hole in the cart, where they can be fastened with a bit of clay.

The reins are black string.

Note how the body of the cart was carefully cut away at the top to give the cart interior room.

The wheels came from an old watch, but you can make them out of cardboard.

Now how about the driver? Take a whole peanut kernel and break it apart gently so that the tiny piece at the top of the kernel, which extends across both halves, does not break off. When you get a half with the little piece intact, press the bottom of that half kernel into a bit of clay on the floor of the cart.

MUSEUM

A peanut man, wearing a hat with a narrow brim, is working in his outdoor museum.

He has saved the bones of a fish from his last fishing trip and has painted them snow white.

A couple of weed-stem poles hold the skeleton. Everything is set in dependable modeling clay.

Once the museum is what he wants it to be he will probably charge admission to it.

FISHERMEN

You already know from making the Racer (page 75) how to use half a kernel. How very cold these men look. Also, the fish don't seem to be biting, which would help to make them look glum.

First fix up your stage using a piece of shiny metal or a mirror for a floor. Line the back part of the stage floor with clay, about an inch wide, and make up a wild shoreline. This will take time but it will be worthwhile doing well.

Now for the boat, which is perhaps the most difficult part. With the little shears level off the bottom of the boat until it stands easily. Next cut out the top part and remove the insides. Now place your men into it. You might have to level off the bottom ends of the half kernels, and you will probably need a bit of clay to stand them up in.

The oars are toothpicks cut short. The fishing rods, which could be feather shafts or most anything, are wire in this case. The rest is easy.

A mirror will make a double image at the bottom of the boat, which polished metal will not, but the double image might suggest that the boat is swaying slightly.

COWBOY

This picture is true to life. When I was fifteen years old, I came home from a rodeo one day and decided I could throw a steer just like the cowboys.

Well, you see what happened. The steer threw me!

The steer is made of a Brazil-nut body and hazelnut head. The horns are feather-shaft tips. The strawstack is steel wool.

The fence is made up of dry stems broken to small pieces and stuck in clay.

You'll know how to do the rest.

SQUIRREL AND OWL

In this arrangement the owl is landing at her nest just in the nick of time to save her eggs. Now that the squirrel has found the eggs, and if he doesn't get a beating from the owl, he will watch for another chance to get those eggs.

The old tree is a piece of driftwood but any piece of branch from 1½ to 2 inches in diameter can be made to do. Saw halfway into one end—about 2 inches from the actual end of the piece, and chip out an opening. This will be covered with steel wool, which is used for the nest.

The eggs are the size of small peas. Anything round, even small beans, can be used but should be painted white.

The owl as well as the squirrel is a whole peanut. The wings and horns are maple seeds. The eyes are small white paper discs with pinheads for pupils. The legs and talons are bits of electrical cord with the insulation removed at the feet, where the thin copper wires are spread out.

The squirrel's tail was carved out of foam rubber, but there are bushy grass heads to be found which would be even better. The squirrel's legs are bits of pipe cleaner.

You will find good use for pipe cleaners so it would be wise to have some on hand. See photo below.

MT. RUSHMORE

Here two kids are working on their own Mt. Rushmore--the mountain with the faces of four great Americans carved into its side.

How do you begin to make a face? You use an egg. The thin end of the egg becomes the chin.

Draw a line across one side of the egg right through the middle. You have to use your judgment about the middle. This line leaves one half of the egg in the heavier, thicker end, and one half in the smaller end.

Now draw another line just halfway between the first line and the chin. Between these two lines come the eyes, nose, and ears.

Draw a third line through the middle of the area which still remains. The mouth comes between the second and third lines.

Now fashion some eyes out of clay and place them on the egg. Make a nose and set it in place, and a good chin, too. Make lips and put them on. Also, show the hairline on the forehead. Now spread very thin clay over the rest of the white space of the egg which remains.

The egg will not spoil in one or two days. If you can't finish the job in that time, put what you have finished into a box and find a place for it in the refrigerator when you are not working on it. This will help preserve the egg.

STRING OF FISH

This peanut man, with his feather-shaft rod and string of fish, is on his way home, taking a shortcut through the meadow because it's getting late. Soon it will be too dark to see.

You'll probably understand how to make everything but the string of fish.

What would you use for a string of fish? I asked myself that question for weeks—long after I had everything else made up as I wanted it.

Then it occurred to me that as a boy on the farm I had often noticed wheat heads that had been relieved of their kernels by threshing. That was it!

I knew a neighbor who made trips to a farm, and explained to him what I needed. He brought *one* to me! The moral to this story is: If you can't find what you need try to think of some friend who could get it for you.

COVERED WAGON

This wagon takes us to the Western plains in the days of the early settlers and oxen teams.

You will see at once that the top part of the wagon is a whole peanut with the end cut off. Use a No. 2 or No. 7 peanut.

The oxen are made of dry lima beans, with pin legs and horns. The head is a navy bean. The eyes are just black dots. In this photograph the horns throw a shadow over the eyes, which makes it appear that the horns come out of the eyes.

The wheels? What a problem that was. I couldn't find anything ready-made by nature which would be lasting. I could think of round things but always there would be no spokes. Finally I settled for slices of kumquat. But this meant that my precious arrangement would soon break down.

If you are willing to make the spokes, the best way to get wheels is to slice the neck of a No. 1 gourd with a hacksaw.

Run a hole through the center to hold the axle, which could be a dowel or feather shaft or sucker stick or even a twig.

84

JINRIKISHA

Looking at this very unusual picture you wonder how in the world the jinrikisha was made. Actually, it is two ribs and a verte-bra from a salmon steak, which turned up at a restaurant where I was having lunch. One just never knows when an interesting thing may appear.

But it would really be easy to make a jinrikisha with the kind of wheels suggested for the Covered Wagon on page 84. And you could find out about shaves on page 133, where they are hooked on Santa's sleigh.

You can figure out how to make the coolie's hat.

His arms and legs are made from heavy paper clips. If you use the long-nose pliers you can twist the ends of the wires to represent hands and feet.

As you work on a project like this you are bound to get ideas of your own. Try them out.

FATHER AND SON FISHING

I consider this one of the best peanut arrangements in the book. However, I am prejudiced, because it reminds me of the first fishing trip on which my father took me. I was four.

The background forest is steel wool with a few weed stalks stuck in for tree trunks.

The bank was carefully laid out to make a special, safe place for the boy to fish. The stump the father's sitting on is clay, too.

The whole thing is built on a shiny piece of metal. You could use a mirror.

The boy, a Spanish peanut, has just caught a fish, and his father won't help him because he wants his boy to learn for himself.

Think about some incident in your own life and work it out. You will be surprised at what you can accomplish.

SHEEP

Here, as with the oxen of the Covered Wagon, page 94, beans are used to construct sheep. Lima beans are the bodies and they have navy-bean heads. The sheep strayed too far from the fold and got themselves marooned on an island, where the farmer found them.

You already know how to arrange your stage with a polished piece of metal or a mirror. The island is, of course, made of modeling clay.

Have you made a hat yet for a peanut man? Cut the tip off of a peanut and paste it on a rounded piece of wrapping paper.

The stick the farmer is carrying is a feather shaft.

The trees are twigs of arborvitae or white cedar, common evergreens that shouldn't be hard to find.

Some weed seeds are scattered along the water's edge.

FISH SHANTY

The shanty is a very dry and thin gourd, with the bottom sawed off. It stands on ice (styrofoam). The man is probably hastening out for more bait.

You could make a whole village of shanties if you wished, but just one will be a trial. This sketch (much to my shame, but to warn you) shows that the saw went too far when I cut out a square for a window. I left some bad marks on the shanty, which show crude workmanship.

Notice how the bend in the arms and legs creates a sense of hurry in the man.

FUNNY PAGE I

To do a series of cartoonlike scenes requires some study, some looking ahead. If you have a little story in mind, work it over carefully and jot down what you want in each picture so that you will have a continuing development of the idea as you work it out.

Here is a scout camp. The leader asks two boys to carry a note to a Mr. Chesterton at a nearby lake. It's probably about arranging for a canoe trip for the boys.

The boys get lost in the woods. They see a man sitting on a log, and ask their way.

The interesting point in the story is that the man tells them that Mr. Chesterton has a dog who hates boys but likes girls.

The boys make themselves skirts to trick the dog into thinking they are girls.

What the boys didn't think of is that the dog could easily see through the whole thing.

This is a lot of fun. You will know by now how to work out the whole thing, though it may seem to take a long time. But it's worth keeping at. Do the first scene and set it aside for a while, then continue with the second, and so on. In other words, find something to do between times to keep your mind fresh for your main project.

91

GROUNDHOG HUNT

Here two boys have chased a groundhog, or woodchuck, into its den and have gotten shovels to dig him out, when their father comes along. He knows about woodchucks, and he tells them they'll never succeed in digging him out. The den is too long, and it usually has two escape doors hidden somewhere.

The dogs seem to understand. They have probably gone through all this many times before.

How to make a dog is on page 141.

The scene here is near a stream. So start with a piece of metal or a mirror.

You can already make the man and the boys. Here, as on several other occasions, you may have noticed that the man has his shirt open at the neck. You can accomplish this with a few careful snips of the little shears.

The tree here is a carrot. For permanence you should use a piece of heavy cornstalk or a branch of a tree.

The unique and new thing is the shovels, which are small squares of paper pasted to toothpicks.

94

THIRSTY BUFFALO

A buffalo (bison) is made much the same way as the steer in Cowboy, page 77: Brazil-nut body, hazelnut head, feather-shaft horns. The long hair around the neck can be made with corn-silk or steel wool or whatever else you may think of.

Here the buffalo comes to the watering trough for a drink. The trough is the hull of a pea. Several peas outside the hull suggest a rocky spot in the buffalo's pasture.

Again a weed tree helps to make the picture interesting.

Beauty, balance, and other artistic values are often brought out best by keeping an arrangement like this very simple. Look at the picture again—there's no annoying detail. It's all done in solid and distinct units.

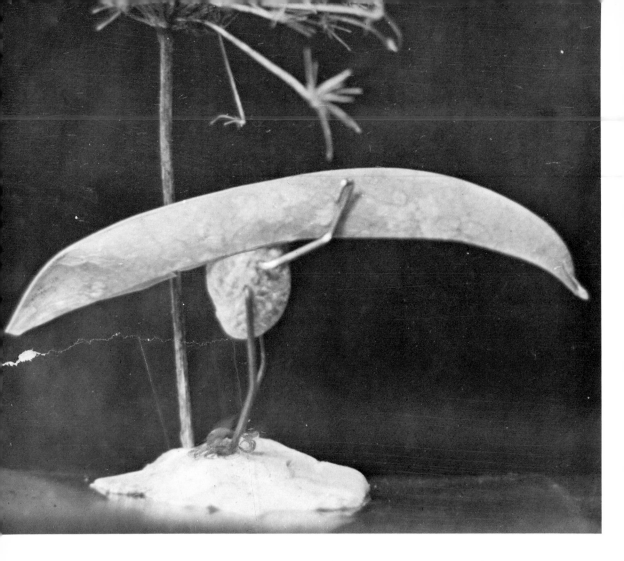

MAN AND CANOE

Read the last paragraph of Thirsty Buffalo again and study this picture with it in mind. Its simplicity is obvious.

Fishermen who fish in wilderness streams often have to carry their canoes around dangerous stretches of rough water. This is called a portage.

This man is making a portage. His canoe—perhaps you have guessed it—is the hull of a pea, nature's perfect replica of a canoe. You already know how to do the man, the island, and the weed tree.

TRAINER

What do you see first in this picture of the Trainer? The giraffe? Its head? Its body? Its legs? Its feet? Look it over well.

The head is a grapefruit seed. The body is a one-kernel peanut. The legs and neck are feather shafts. The feet are bits of cornstalk. The tail is part of a feather.

This giraffe is a well-built animal. It can stand on a solid floor without the help of clay.

The trainer is the standard peanut man. His long staff is a feather shaft.

FUNNY PAGE II

Here the boys are in the woods with their dog, who has chased a woodchuck into a tree.

The dog crawls right into the hollow tree, and soon the boys are afraid their pet is hopelessly stuck. They do not know that there is an underground passage to the stump.

Fluffy comes out behind the boys and scares them off their feet. One jumps up high while the other falls to the ground.

This would be an interesting winter project for you. We learn to do by doing, and we learn how by first following a model.

After you have done one or both of these sets of funny scenes, you may want to do a set of your own. If you do a good job you might want to exhibit it at school or somewhere else in town.

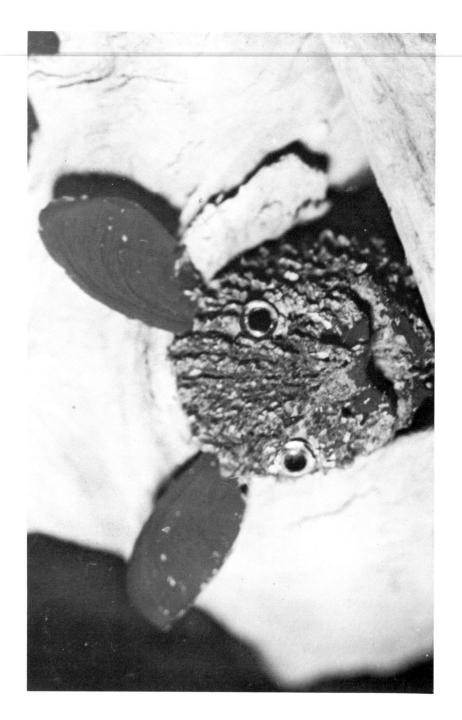

A BEAR AWAKENS

Bears hibernate through winter months. When they wake up in the spring, I wonder if they wear a look of surprise at the world outside of their cave or den. They surely must.

Examine some black walnuts. At one end you will find a sort of point. At the other end a walnut often has a mass of hardened pulp, which can be scratched off. This is the end of the nut to be used for the nose and mouth. If there isn't enough pulp to scratch away to make a natural mouth and nose, you may have to use a little black paint as I did.

Use large eyes if you have some on hand. If you can't make them stick on the rough ridges of the nut, fill the ridges with a bit of clay, but don't let the clay show from under the eyes. Use a little glue on the eyes before you place them.

RIDER

To appreciate the Rider a little more turn back to the Racer, p. 75. You will see that it is the same horse, except that the legs have been changed to give it a different gait. The head is the most interesting part of the horse, a grapefruit seed. Grapefruit seeds seem never to be alike so one has to hunt sometimes through everybody's breakfast remains to find just the right shape.

While there is a band around the horse, the rider is actually riding bareback.

The rider is a Spanish peanut. But these are hard to find, and a regular-size peanut rider would make the horse look like a pony.

There is a solution. Peanuts frequently have one end undeveloped. The shell is there but no kernel. Careful use of your little shears might make this small end of the peanut right for the body of the rider.

The peculiar tree in the background is a weed.

EAGLES NEST

This arrangement has always intrigued me. There's the big nest. Both boys want to know what's in it. One of them gets up enough courage to find out, while the other waits eagerly to see what his friend will discover.

The trees here are parsnips, which are good to eat, so we must remove them soon from the scene. But how about using the roots of something else, which we do not consider food, like a big stalk of Queen Anne's lace (wild carrot).

However, if you are aiming at a permanent display you'd better use branch parts, or cornstalk, or sunflower stalks for your trees.

The nest is steel wool. Weed parts are stuck around in clay.

106

PLAYGROUND SLIDE

This picture introduces a very interesting product from nature, the bean of a catalpa tree.

The slide is just half of such a bean with one end cut off. By all means examine one of these beans the next chance you get. They fall in late summer. Empty the inside and you have a very smooth slide, which could be used in transporting many things such as water at a well, grain, coal at a mine.

The kids here are made of Spanish peanuts. The presence of a full-grown man makes them look like children. Note how their legs are bent.

The ladder is made of feather shafts and the rounds are thin spaghetti.

The dog was carved out of foam rubber, but could be of most anything.

FEEDING DONKEY

This is a great one to do. It's tough but just follow directions and you'll make it.

Here is what you will need: (1) a Brazil nut with a good forehead for a donkey, (2) a piece of thin cornstalk or dowel or sucker stick, (3) part of one side of a feather, (4) a piece of cornstalk for a neck, (5) ears; if maple seeds are not available cut the ears out of thin cardboard; cut them in one piece, (6) a piece of cardboard maple seed or the real thing, (7) one eye, (8) modeling clay.

The delicate part is the saw cuts. If you have a vise tighten the nut in it but do not crack the nut. Hold it steady with one hand while you make the saw cuts. Make the cut for the ears. Also, while the nut is still in this position make a cut back of the forehead, then another to meet it, so that you can chip out a triangle. You may need a small bit to clean out the triangle so there is a hole big enough for the dowel or thin cornstalk. Now turn the nut and make a cut where the mouth is to be.

Make a slot in the cornstalk piece to be used for the neck. Make it big enough so that you can slide it on the dowel from the top. Use clay to fasten it in place. Now fasten the piece of feather with clay.

You will need an extra stage back. Cut a window into this. Fit the donkey into the window and decide how long the dowel will have to be to fit through a hole you must make in the back stage wall. (It wouldn't matter, of course, if the dowel sticks out at the back.) The neck of the donkey should rest on the window bottom or sill. Paint the cornstalk neck the color of the nut head rather than dappled like mine.

109

HENS ON A ROOST

It doesn't take very much imagination to see in these 12 single-kernel peanuts a flock of hens sitting on the roost, their heads tucked under their wings.

The framework of the roost is all made of the top section of cornstalk—that which has the tassel on it. You'll discover what a marvelous material cornstalk is to work with.

Notice that some pins are showing. Pins push easily into cornstalk. There are three posts in the back with a crosspiece over them, and three rafters that hold the roof. All of these are held together with pins. The two supporting cornstalks are also pinned to the rest of the framework.

To make the hens sit I ran a wire through them. Perhaps the best wire for this would be a piece of light coat hanger. The wire florists use would also work.

Be sure you string your hens on the wire "facing" you or they may not look like hens.

Note the little drinking trough on the ground, which is a piece of cornstalk hollowed out.

Roof and sidewalls will be easy for you. I suggest using corrugated cardboard such as cartons are made of.

MAILBOXES

A tall, long-faced man has gone to get his mail. Three other box holders have not yet gotten theirs.

Nobody keeps the weeds cut around the mailboxes.

The fencelike boards that hold the mailboxes are emery boards, which were stapled together.

The mailboxes were balanced on the top rail. This could easily be done by cutting a slot in the bottom of the nut with your shears. Or, you could staple two emery boards together with a bit of cardboard at either end to hold the boards apart so that they would easily balance a peanut.

TUMBLEBUG

As a boy on the farm I watched the tumblebug along back lanes rolling his big ball to make it bigger. Some balls were an inch in diameter.

The bug lays its eggs into bits of food that the young will live on for a while when they first hatch, then rolls it all up in a ball the size of a walnut. The young will eventually eat their way out.

After a long time of thinking about it I found that an almond kernel would serve well as the bug's body, but I had to paint it black.

I cut and tore parts of the plume off rather small feathers to make the legs.

Now what to use for a ball! I found it under a sycamore tree. This creation would last for many months.

This, again, is a reminder to keep your eyes open for nature's free craft supplies. There is no end to them.

113

114

SLEEPING STUDENT

This student was so tired he fell into bed with his hat on.

First of all, note the log wall and beginning of the attic ceiling. These logs are made of the sections at the top of the cornstalk, which are smooth and easy to work with.

The pennant could say almost anything, and you can figure out how to make the student. Notice how he keeps his arms up as he sleeps.

The bed is the most interesting thing in this room. It is all made of the top sections of cornstalk. Some of it is flattened to make it look more like boards. The oversize mattress is a piece of sponge rubber, or you can use another soft material.

It's easy to make a bed like this. Everything is stuck together with ordinary pins. The two pins nearest the center of the side board hold slats, which keep the whole frame steady as well as hold the mattress. There is one center upright post just above the student's head, which makes three in all for the headboard. There are only two for the footboard.

WATCH BIRD

Perhaps this bird should be called a lady bird because it is made up of hairpins and hatpins.

If an old pocket watch happens to be around, why not have the bird see what time it is?

The maple-seed wings add a lot to the picture, and by now you will know how to attach them, and the big eye, too.

Study the picture carefully and you will be able to make it without further instructions. Probably a No. 2 or No. 7 peanut would be best for the watch bird.

BIRDS FEEDING

The birds' wings are the broadest part of the biggest maple seeds you can find.

The birds' bodies are single-kernel peanuts.

See how the peanuts are turned to show a small natural beak. (This is the end that opens to let the kernel germinate when the seed is put in the ground.)

Long weed stems and a dark background set off the birds.

The birds are pinned on several of the heavier weed stems. (You can see one of the pins.)

The selection of nuts is very important. Look every one over very carefully before you decide which are best for a particular activity.

118

CORN SHOCK AND PUMPKIN

The easiest way to make a corn shock is to make a foundation and place stalks against it. Use a cone-shaped paper cup.

The top piece of the foundation should have a hole in the bottom so grass heads can be pushed through it to make them stand. Fasten the two paper parts together with tape. They may not fit perfectly, but that is not important. Set this form on a thin cake of clay so the stalks that stand against it will have their feet anchored in the clay.

I used the seed heads of long grasses, both for stalks and for the tassels at the top. When the paper is well covered, tie up the shock at the slender center part of the foundation.

The pumpkin is a black walnut. I made a small pancake out of clay, put it over the nut, then rolled it in my hands until the whole nut was covered. To make the grooves in the pumpkin, fold a piece of cardboard, stick a finger inside the folded part and draw it across the pumpkin from top to bottom. I painted my pumpkin bright orange.

Set this on your stage and you will get some ideas for more projects.

Part V Variety Studies

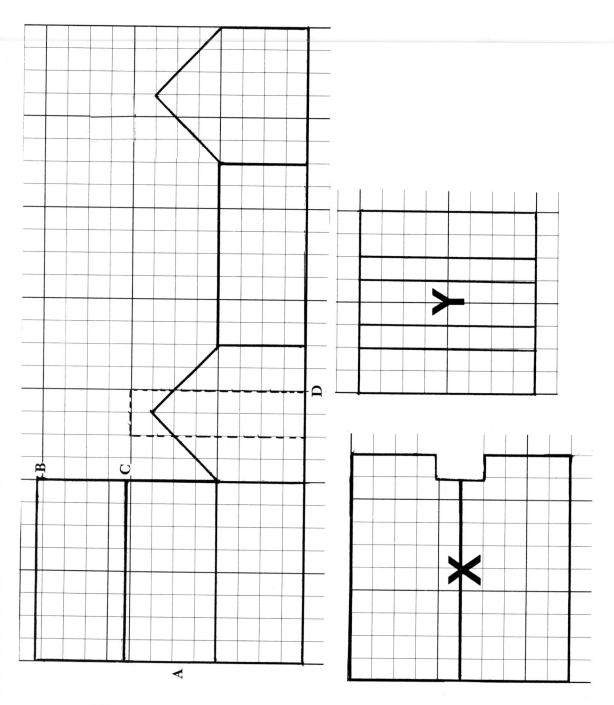

CABIN

The best way to get the dimensions of the cabin right is to use a sheet of graph paper marked out in quarter-inch squares. Count the squares in the diagram and mark them on your sheet of quarter-inch squares so that you can make the same outline. Use a ruler to make the lines.

The outside line, A, on the left must measure $3\frac{3}{16}$ inches. Note that two horizontal lines, B and C, are not drawn right on the lines of the squares. You will know why later.

The bottom line, D, must be 7 inches long, or 28 squares. Now study the rest of the outline and proceed to finish your drawing. When all the lines are in and your sketch looks exactly like the one in the book, use a sheet of carbon paper and transfer your lines to a piece of lightweight cardboard. Now cut your outline out along the outside lines only.

Now score the two horizontal lines B and C and the remaining upright lines. Bend all these back, and be sure that you make a sharp fold in each case. This is best done by flattening one side over another and running your ruler over the crease.

You will now be able to put the cabin walls and roof together. Fasten them down with cellophane tape.

By now you will be able to figure out how to do the chimney, Y. Glue the chimney in place. Next comes the fitting of the roof, X. Here you must make sure to push the notch in the roof tightly against the chimney.

There are many things you can do with your cabin. Probably

you will want windows and a door, and you can paint it to look like a log cabin. Perhaps you will make a summer scene on your stage—a beautiful grove with flowers and trees.

I made a winter scene out of mine, but I wish I had turned the chimney side out as it is in the photograph above. The tree is a cone. The supply of firewood outside is running low. A tiny path runs to the lake where a hole was cut in the ice for water.

Making snow will be a problem. Clay can be used and later painted white, but it will be difficult and will take a lot of patience. Cotton might be more to your liking. Just keep trying and you will be sure to find a way to create a beautiful scene.

126

DANCERS

This makes a marvelous floral centerpiece for the dinner table. You'll have to get it all ready before you pick the snapdragons. (Perhaps large pansies would work, and there may be other flowes. I'm for snapdragons because of the motion supplied by the raised "arm" as well as the skirt.)

First, set your stage. Have the dancers up on a higher plane than the fence.

Second, have large pins or wires ready, with small balls of clay for heads. Stick one in place and measure a flower to see if you have the length right. However, if the clay beneath is thick enough you can do a lot of regulating.

Third, make a fence at the front of the stage with broken pieces of dry weed stem. Don't make a fancy stage; it would distract from the dancers.

Now you are ready for the gowns. Keep them fresh until the very last minute. Stick the head pin or wire through the back side of the flower and stand it up in the clay base.

The family will appreciate this display.

SAILBOAT

Suppose you are about to go on a vacation trip to a lake and wonder what you can do if you get tired of swimming, since you've had to leave your gourd projects at home. Well, here's a chance to tie your craft work to your vacation.

Take a walk along the beach away from the water and look for seagull feathers. Next try the wooded areas. You may find a fallen birch tree or at least a large branch of one.

Cut off a piece of bark lengthwise from the log or branch. The curve of the log or branch will remain in the piece you cut off. This is the important point in making a sail. The curve of the trunk or branch will put "wind" in the sail. (See sketch.)

Keep your eyes open for a small piece of driftwood, or even a piece of bark.

Cut a hole in one end of the piece of driftwood for the mast. Use the feather shaft for a mast. Fasten the bark to it with sewing thread, if that is the handiest, or a bit of nylon fishline.

The sailboat we made from our findings is still around. We are proud of it. It has memories for us.

If you can't make the sailboat on the spot, take home the things you have collected for it and finish it there.

(In the photograph the sail is pulled in to get a complete view of the project. If you were out sailing and had the sail in this position, you would move sideways. Perhaps you can figure out a way to make a boom.)

CHRISTMAS GARDEN

When the festivities of Christmas are over and you wonder
what to do with yourself, take the cones, pine needles, nuts, etc.,
and make a garden.

I used Brazil nuts to throw together a fence. Cones went for
trees. Pine needles helped out.

I didn't get to spend much time on this one, but enough to
give you an idea. Make a beautiful winter garden for the family
to enjoy.

SANTA

Here's a construction that needs patience to do, but it's packed with pleasure.

First let's see what all the parts are, and then we'll put them together:

1. The reindeer is a No. 1 gourd, but has a bumpy outside. Pulling a paintbrush over the bumpy sides, I made it look like heavy fur. 2. The head is a very small, almost egg-shaped gourd. If perhaps you can't find one, then use a pecan nut or whatever else you may think of. 3. The antlers are weeds. 4. Below the neck is a part of a feather. 5. The legs are cornstalk. 6. The tail is clay. 7. The shaves that hook the reindeer to the sleigh are wire (such as florists use), which has a twist at the U end that is shoved into a hole in the sleigh. 8. The strap around the deer's body that holds the shaves is cornhusk. 9. The reins are spaghetti. 10. The runners on the sleigh are candles, attached to the sleigh with cornstalk braces. 11. The sleigh is a No. 7 gourd like the owl. 12. Santa is a gourd with cornhusk hat and white feathers for hair. 13. The sleigh is packed with nuts and gourds.

Now, what's hard about it? What haven't you yet done? The candles! They are 18 inches long when straight. Hold them in warm water until they bend as you see them in the picture.

You can figure out the cuts in the gourd body of the sleigh. You will use the saw. When these cuts are made, clean out the interior of the sleigh.

To get a good idea of the legs of the deer go back to the camel.

This would make a very attractive centerpiece for the Christmas dinner table.

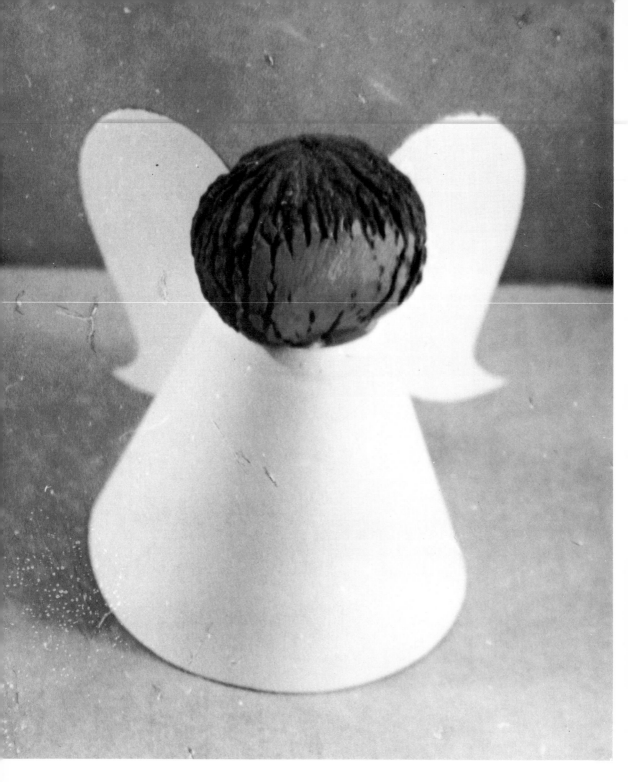

CHUBBY CHERUB

Look at the diagram picture to see what we are after here. It is one of the most interesting constructions this book has to offer.

Again, you need a piece of graph paper that is ruled in quarter-inch squares. But in this case the outline will not be as simple to follow as the outlines for the cabin were.

First you have to draw the curved line, A, at the bottom of the top design; then the shorter curved line, B, at the top, just 2 inches from the bottom one. If you find a way to draw these curves you can count the squares and find where the outer corners of each curve stop.

When you have this drawn on lightweight cardboard, cut it out and bring the ends together. This will form the skirt for Chubby. The dotted line shows the overlap. Secure the ends with glue. See photo of rear view of Chubby on page 136.

The wings are more difficult. Draw one and then fold the cardboard and cut around this first one, but be sure you leave about a half inch between. Paste it on the skirt.

You are now probably wondering about the head and face. What can you find to make a good head?

Turning to nature is the best choice here. The design of Chubby is so simple that it is beautiful, and a natural material will be in keeping with Chubby's artistic simplicity.

 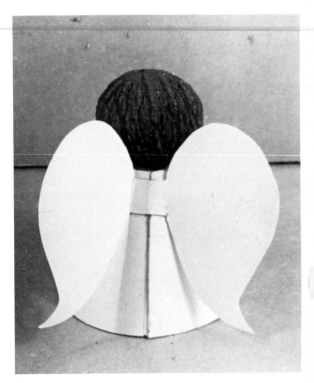

I have not tried an English walnut, but I have used a black walnut. I put the nut in the vise and filed away enough of the rough edge to make a face. Paint and eyes I think would spoil it, so I left it plain.

There is one other nut that has a natural face—the horse chestnut. Horse chestnuts come in pairs in a pod, sometimes three, but usually two. Each has a light-colored "face," while all the rest is a rich chestnut brown. But this surface is shiny and smooth, while the black walnut does much better to simulate natural hair for Chubby.

The next problem is to anchor the head if you think it should be on solid. Double-stick tape is the answer, but you will have to experiment in the use of it. It will be hard not to let it show on the outside.

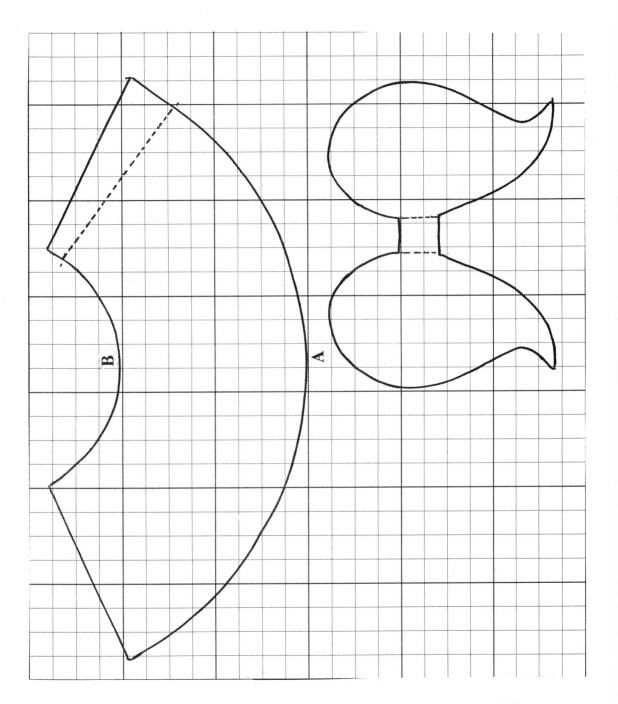

APPENDIX

RUBBER DOG

You have seen several dogs in my displays, and you wonder how they were made. It is perhaps a little more difficult than making a peanut man, but this is how they were done.

Sketch an outline of the size dog you want. Hunt till you find a picture of one that size. If it's on heavy paper use tracing paper to trace off the outline. (Tissue paper will do in a pinch.)

When you have the outline, use carbon paper to transfer it onto a piece of foam rubber, usually known at craft stores as "art foam" or "fashion foam." Use foam of a quarter-inch thickness.

Now clip out the dog right over the outline, using your little shears. This done you are off to a good start. Now round off all corners and clip away between the front and rear legs. If this makes the legs wobbly you will have to hide a pin in them.

Keep up the clipping until you have a dog that you like. Glass eyes would perhaps be better than my painted ones, but you may have to attach them with rubber cement.

INTRODUCTION TO THE AUTHOR

R.E. Eshmeyer was born May 2, 1898 near New Knoxville, Ohio. Much of his youth was spent on farms, where nature became his constant companion. After graduation from the New Bremen, Ohio High School in 1916 he taught school for a year, edited and printed a house organ for a local department store another year, then enrolled in the Student Army Training Corps at Heidelberg College, Tiffin, Ohio. While at Heidelberg he chose the Christian Ministry as his profession, and later took his theological training at Central Theological Seminary at Dayton, Ohio.

A one-hour art course at Heidelberg developed in him an interest in painting and in chalk talks. This interest turned out to serve him well in the ministry, for during the forty years in that profession he gave approximately 1000 chalk talks to church and civic groups, and taught classes in oil painting to church groups, and, over a period of thirty years, devoted his summer vacations to teaching oil painting to a total of some 4000 high school and college students at Camp Miniwanca in western Michigan.

Along the way he developed an interest in plaster-of-Paris modeling, and, among other things, prepared models of 123 species of fish for Heidelberg and another 97 for Purdue University. 150 face masks, too, were made of members of the congregations he served in Cleveland, Akron and Lansing, and his students at camp. In Lansing a unique Christmas creche was displayed on the church grounds, using discarded mannequins with plaster-of-Paris masks of young people selected annually by the church youth group.

Among his other achievements is a collection of 176 species of Ohio trees for Heidelberg college. A more recent interest in photography developed into pictures of table-top nature scenes, which were published in the Lansing State Journal under the title, "Hobby Shop Zoo." Many of these appear in this book.

In this book a gourd becomes a lamp, a rabbit with maple-seed ears, a flower pot, penguins, other birds, a camel, an owl, a grasshopper, a nesting hen. A yam becomes a rooster with onion-skin tail, a seal, sealions. Peanuts become people, birds, a hen roost, a racer, a fisherman, a cowboy. Two rib bones and a vertebra of a salmon become a ginricksha. A peanut horse has a grapefruit-seed head. Half a catalpa bean becomes a schoolyard slide. A threshed wheat head becomes a string of fish. Snapdragons become dancers. A peanut man carries a pea-hull canoe. And many others.

While the author sticks close to nature he is not completely purist, for he includes plans for making a cabin with paper, a paper cherub, carved rubber dogs, a sailboat, and others.

When he was asked how he got started on the 150 or so projects in this book he didn't really know. "I suppose," he said, "they must have begun with Christmas and Easter displays for the church school. When these seemed to go over I took pictures of

144

them and brought them to the local newspaper. When they were accepted here I began to realise that, as in the case of chalktalks, I had come upon something which would help along the sort of public-relations idea I had, as well as catch the interest of children who happened to see the pictures."

Today, at 76, he's still at it, using free craft materials from the ever unlimited supply—nature. He even collects "weeds" in the winter time.

His popular Sunday morning Junior Sermons, using a nature story with a biblical interpretation, and designed to appeal to young people, were carried as a regular feature in the Sunday edition of the Lansing State Journal for several years. More recently he published a volume of poems entitled, "It Crossed My Mind."

His love and concern for his fellowman enabled him to serve in various other capacities as well—among them was an eight-year term on the Heidelberg Board of Trustees, an orphanage Board, and various civic, Church Council and denominational committees.

Here then we have a minister, a naturalist, a photographer, a poet and an artist with broad humanitarian interests who, in a unique way, has used his talents to contribute to the happiness and well being of his fellowmen, and to make his own life, especially in his retirement years, more meaningful.

Kermit V. Ohl
Lansing, Michigan

INDEX